POGO

BY WALT KELLY

SIMON AND SCHUSTER · NEW YORK

FABLE OF CONTENTS

*It should be borne in mind that at the time *we* were study-
ing *bats, bats* had an excellent opportunity to study *us*.

DISCLAIMER

Most books are dedicated to some person—a friend, relative, customer, sweetheart, animal, vegetable, or mineral. It would, however, be unjust to fix the responsibility for the material herein contained on anyone in particular.

Practically everybody that Kelly knows or has ever met is equally guilty. His own mother is not entirely blameless. She early aided and abetted him, never broke him to the muzzle or the leash. His father, an otherwise virtuous man, taught him how to draw. His sister sharpened his pencils and corrected his spelling. These misdemeanors were compounded by later associates, many of whom, masquerading as school teachers, encouraged him in a shameless manner. Newspapermen, artists, writers, and Hollywood animators taught him the rudiments of anti-social behavior until he became fit for nothing but comic strip work.

As a result, it should be stressed that the fault here lies not so much with Kelly, who is merely an easily influenced youth on the sunny side of thirty-nine, but with his associates, early and late. It should be further stressed that Kelly's companions being what they are, most of them have been late most of the time.

Speaking for himself (a steady habit of his), Kelly declines to be responsible (another steady habit) for this exhibition.

A WOMAN HAS ONLY ACUMEN

BUT A GOOD CIGAR IS A SMOKE

1

2

3

6

A Mere Meanwhile away.

WELL! IF IT ISN'T THE REAL McGEE, THE SUBSTITUTE MAIL MAN.

UNCLE REGULAR CURTIS IS SICK --- GOT A LETTER FO' YOU, ALBERT.

READ IT SOME.

LET'S SEE - FIRST WE GOT A "X" OR POSSIBLE A "B". THEM "B" BOYS CREEPS IN EV'YWHERE. GOTTA WATCH 'EM --- THEN A COUPLE "R'S" AN' A PASSEL OF LI'L BITTY THINGS LIKE ANTS.

PHOO! THAT ALL THE READIN' YOU GONE DO?

WHAT YOU WANTS FROM 'THE CIVIL SERVICE? SINGIN' AN' DANCIN'?

ALBERT! ALBERT! WONDERFUL NEWS!!

I GOT ALL THE NEWS I CAN STAND BUT I CAN'T READ IT.

8

I BET I IS *RAVISHIN'* FIT TO KILL!

WARN THE GENTRY! THE *PEST HOUSE* MUST OF IS DONE *BUST LOOSE!*

A HIGH CLASS GAL LIKE STRAWBERRY SHORTCUT WILL WANT YOU TO GIVE UP SEEGARS SO I WILL JUS' HOLD THE BOX.

HERE SHE COME!

EL FALFA 20 for 5¢

HOT DOG! THEY IS *BOTH* SPEECHLESS!

H'LO THERE, BIG BOY. I IS STRAWBERRY SHORTCUT, THE BATON ROUGE BOMB SHELL-- WHY DON'T YOU GIVE UP SEEGARS?

GOOD WORK, POGO!

JUS' A MINUTE, BROWN EYES-- I GONE SIGN THE PLEDGE 'GAINST SMOKIN'.

MAN! I IS A *NATURAL BORN SYREEN.*

11

HOW *MICE* OF YOU TO DROP IN

AN INSIDE STORY

14

15

17

19

21

SCIENCE ALWAYS FINDS A WAY! PSYCHOL OWOGGY WILL ROUSE THEM LI'L OL' MICE OUTEN YO' INNARDS, ALBERT.

GOT AS MUCH RIGHT HERE AS ANY-BODY.

ROGER! THAT'S ME.

I'VE TRAINED ROGER TO DEECOY THEM OUT. HE'LL TALK 'EM INTO LEAVIN' ----- GO IT, ROGER!

HEY! IT'S ROGER! GREAT! NOW WE'VE GOT A FOURTH. CUT THE CARDS, CHARLES.

WHOSE DEAL?

DON'T FEEL BAD, OWL. IT'S BETTER'N THEM PLAYIN' HIDE AND SEEK. MAN! ALL THAT OL' RUNNIN' AROUND! THEY GOT THE COLDEST LITTLE FEET THIS SIDE OF LAPLAND!

STILL, ROGER DISAPPOINTS ME.

SCIENCE WILL FIND A WAY! JUSTICE WILL TRIUMPH! I WILL GET 'EM OUT.

HERE Y'ARE, ALBERT! OPEN WIDE. MAN! THIS GONE BE LIKE SHOOTIN' FISH IN A BARREL.

IF THEM MICE WON'T COME OUT ANY OTHER WAY, ALBERT, WE'LL *TRAP* 'EM!

GOOD! I HEARD 'IT CLICK ON *SOMETHIN'*!

ONLY THING YOU GOT WAS MY *SEEGAR*.

PHOO! JUST IN TIME! WE QUIT! YOU SMOKED US OUT! WE CAN'T STAND NO MORE OF YO' SEEGARS.

LET'S GO BACK TO THAT JOB WE HAD IN THE NURSERY RHYME ~~~~

HICKORY DICKORY, *PARLEZ-VOUS?*

FOUR-FLUSHING
The
GROUND HOG
FROM COVER TO COVER

27

28

29

TRY ON THAT OL' **FUR CAP**, POGO, IT'S A *KEEPSAKE* LEFT BEHIND BY A OL' RACKETY-COON ASSOCIATE --- AN' THAT BONE BEIN' PRESSED IN THE BOOK IS IN MEMORY OF MY FIRST FORMAL **HOT DOG** ROAST.

COME! WE'LL FIND A **GROUND HOG**! HE'LL END OUR DILEMMA. THAT LI'L SAGACIOUS SEER WILL TELL US IF WINTER'S END IS AT HAND.

AND WHO CAN BEST FIND A GROUND HOG? WHO, INDEED, BUT MAN'S BEST FRIEND, THE NOBLE DOG. HE IS WISE AND KEEN OF MIND, ALERT AND READY, QUICK TO ---- *WELL, HALLO!* HOW'D **YOU** LIKE TO HELP LOCATE A GROUND HOG?

GLAD TO! I'M A NATURAL BORN WOOD-CHUNK MYSELF.

GOOD FOR YOU!

THE DOG'S AMAZING MEMORY RECALLS A TIMELY VERSE: HOW MUCH WOOD WOULD A WOOD CHUNK CHUNK WOULD A WOOD CHUNK CHUNK WOULD A WOOD CHUNK CHUNK WOODAWOOD WUNK CHUNK WOODA WOO WA WUH WOZZA, HUM?'

GREAT! OR: HOW MUCH GROUND ROUND WOULD A HOUND DOG HOG IF A GROUND HOG WAS ROUND GROUND?

A WOOD CHUNK!

31

SOME OLD EGGS IN A NEW BASKET

WE IS GONNA MARCH ON *WASHINGTON* AND DEMAND TO SEE THE *EASTER BUNNY.*

WHY? *EASTER* ISN'T HERE.

BUT WE IS! AN' WE WANTS TO MAKE SURE OUR PUBLIC SERVANTS IS---

--*AS READY AS US!*

THAT'S SURE EXORCISIN' YOUR CIVIL RIGHTS.

IT'S A CRY AN' SHAME--- OL' *EASTER BUNNY* IS *NOWHERE* ROUND --- I WILL PERSONAL *DRESS* UP LIKE THE RABBIT IN A OL' *BUNNY* SUIT I WEARS ON COLD NIGHTS.

ALBRT

CAN'T JES' LEAVE THE CHILLUN GO WITHOUT *EASTER EGGS---* SAY WHERE DO THE OL' BUNNY *GIT* THEM EGGS?

STRONG OL' LEGEND SAY HE PLAIN *LAYS 'EM* PERSONAL.

Albert

39

HOW TO THANK ALBERT? *I KNOW*, WE'LL BE LIKE *CROCODILE* BIRDS WHAT KEEP THE *CROCODILES TEETH CLEAN* BY *PLUCKIN' TIDBITS OUTEN* THEM.

CAREFUL, MIZ GRACKLE, *THAT* IS ALBERT'S *TONGUE*.

WHAT A *PITY*--- IT'S SUCH A *BIG* PIECE.

PLUCK EASY, YOU LI'L' DENTAL HYENAS.

IS YOU THRU PICKIN' ALBERT'S TEETH LIKE A CROCODILE BIRD, MIZ GRACKLE?

YEP AN' LONG AS 'T RAININ', I'LL LEAVE TH' CHILLUN INDOORS AN' I VISITS AUNT PANSY.

GONE SNEEZE! UGH--OOP HUB---- *HUGGEE AH~ AH~*

NOT NOW! NOT NOW!

CHOO!

LOOKY THERE, PANSY! MY LI'L' SHIRT TAIL TADS FLEW OVER BY THEMSELVES *NO HANDS!* AN' WITH LESS FEATHERS 'TWEEN 'EM THAN YOU FIND IN A NEST OF MUD TURKLES

TALENT RUN IN THE FAMBLY.

SOME GENTLEMEN
of the
FOURTH
ESCAPE

44

WHANG! HE FIRES AN' ONE IS DEAD! BLAM! TWO! BANG! ANOTHER! BAM BAM-THREE MORE! WHAM-ONE MORE-BLAM TWO MORE- WHAP-UH-BOO-

GOOD SHOW, CECIL, BLIMEY.

HOLD IT, CECIL --- UP TO NOW YOU IS KILLED OFF YO' ENEMY, YO' GAL, YO' PAL, YO' HOSS, YO' OWN SELF AND FOUR POOR CRITTURS WHAT WASN'T IN THE STORY NOHOW.

TOO MANY, HUH?

GOOD AFTERNOON, YOUNG MAN, I'M A BOOKWORM BY TRADE, READY TO REVIEW A BOOK, RUN ERRANDS OR ANSWER THE TELEPHONE.

OL' ALBERT AN' POGO HAVE A NEWS-PAPER ---- MIGHT BE THEY NEEDS A BOOK-REVIEWER

TAKE THIS BOOK I RIDE ON, IT'S THE WRONG COLOR ---- AND CHEAP AT THAT. SEE, IT RUNS! DOESN'T RESIST WATER.

NOW THIS PAGE CHOSEN AT RANDOM IS LUMPY WITH PUNCTUATION ---- HARD ON THE TEETH --CRAWLING WITH CONSONANTS ----UGH! WHAT SHODDY MATERIAL!

AH, ME! MODERN LITERATURE HAS NO STAYING POWER! SEE, IT WENT DOWN LIKE A STONE.

WHAT WAS THE NAME OF THE BOOK?

OH, WHO KNOWS? I DIDN'T READ THAT FAR.

POGO, I GITTIN' TIRED OF THE NEWSPAPER BUSINESS--- SAY! LET ME TRY THAT!

NO WONDER YOU IS A GOOD SPELLER! YOU GOT A LI'L SPELLIN' MACHINE!

AAH! THIS BLACK-STAGGERED LI'L BLAGGARD IS SNAGGED MY FINGERBONE!

ARRGHFF! YOU BOG STOMPIN' TREECHEROUS LI'L SNEAK! YOU AMBUSHED ME! LEGGO! LEGGO!

WELL, ALBERT, THAT PUTS US OUT OF BUSINESS ALL RIGHT--YOU IS SMASHED OUR ONLY PRESS TO BITS.

AN' NOT ANY TOO SOON! THE FREEDOM OF THAT PRESS GOT SO FAR OUT OF HAND WE MIGHT ALL OF BEEN CON-SOOMED!

HEY, POGO, COME AN' WATCH MY FRIEND THE BOOK WORM, HE'S REVIEWIN' A BOOK FOR YOUR NEWSPAPER.

BUT, WE IS OUT OF BUSINESS.

IT'S JUST AS WELL---THIS BOOK WILL NEVER GET BY-- ITS PACE IS ALL WRONG-- --THE PLOT IS DISJOINTED- --THE CHARACTERS ARE WEAK ITS SPELLING IS BAD!

UPON ATOM

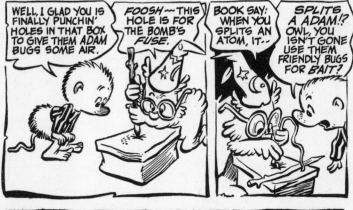

THAT LOOK LIKE A *MIGHTY* SIZEABLE **LUNCH**, POGO --- ROOM FOR AT LEAST **TWO** ----

IT'S *NO LUNCH!* THESE IS THE ADAM BUGS I RESCUES FROM A FIEND WHAT WAS GONE USE 'EM FOR BAIT.

BAIT NOTHIN' -- POGO STOLE MY **ADAMS** OF WHOM I WAS GONE MAKE A BOMB OF.'

HAW! BAIT AN' BOMBS, INDEED! WHAT **BALDY** DASH!

THINK I'LL JES' PLAIN FOLLOW POGO. I *KNOWS* A **LUNCH** BOX WHEN I *BE-HOLES* ONE.

YOU IS RUINED MY LIFE WORK, POGO --- NOW I GOTTA WALK CLEAR HOME FOR ANOTHER **BOX**.

AND, *MAN!* I IS *REALLY* GONE *PACK* **THAT** ONE!

HE SOUND LIKE THE BOY TO FOLLOW.

OL' OWL WAS GONE USE US FOR BAIT? WELL, MEBBE HE WOULD OF SPLIT WITH US.

SPLIT *WITH* YOU? FOOP! HE WOULD OF SPLIT YOUR PERSONALITY *RIGHT* DOWN THE MIDDLE WITH A *BAIT* KNIFE.

BEIN' *BAIT* DON'T PAY --- IT **SPOILS** YOU --- EVEN DO YOU **KETCH** SOMETHIN'.

CAN'T WIN BEIN' BAIT, HUH?

NOPE. BAIT *NEVER* WIN.

OL' OWL CLAIM HE MAKIN' A **ADAM BOMB** --- *HAW HAW* --- HE CAN'T PULL MY WOOL OVER THE ICE --- HE UP TO *SOMETHIN'.*

I B'LEEVE HE'S *PREE*PARIN' A BIG OL' **LUNCH** --- *HAW!* I WILL SPY OUT HIS SECRET -- HE'LL NEVER KNOW ME AS A OL' **SIZZLE GRINDER**.

DOG MY CATS! A HANDSOME MAN LOOKS GOOD IN ANYTHING --- I SHOULD OF BEEN A ACTOR -- *MIGHT OF BEEN ANOTHER* **RING-TING-TING** -- MY *DISGUISE* IS IMPENATRABOBBLE!

H'LO, LI'L FROG TADS.

H'LO, ALBERT--- YOU COTCH YO' HEAD IN A **GRACKLE** NEST?

THERE GO TURTLE, UP TO OWL'S HOUSE. NOW I'LL SEE IF THEY IS TRYIN' TO HIDE SOME GOODIES.

CHURCHY, WE IS GONE MAKE A **ADAM BOMB** ---- IT'S ALL THE RAGE ---- YOU ALL SET TO FIGGER, FELLOW-SINUS?

YEP, I BRINGS MY EE·RASER

58

I KNOWS! I KNOWS! YOU CROSSES 'EM AN' YOU GITS TO THE OTHER SIDE.

HOW *REE-DICULOST!* IF YOU CROSS THESE, *YOU GITS A YEW-RANIUM* BUSH!

HMMPH

WELL, DR. LYSENKO, *WE BEEN WAITIN' HALF A HOUR---* MEBBE IF WE CROSSES OUR FINGERS, TOO?

THE NATURAL BORN REASON WE DIDN'T GIT NO *YEW*-RANIUM WHEN WE CROSSES THE LI'L *YEW* TREE AND THE *GEE*-RANIUM IS *ON* ACCOUNT OF CAUSE WE DIDN'T HAVE NO *GEIGER* COUNTER

WHAT FO' WE *NEEDS* ONE?

TO COUNT THE LI'L GEIGERS, *NATURAL.* TAKE THE COUNTER NOW-- WE TRIES IT AGAIN ----

I READY TO COUNT---CHASE THEM GEIGERS PAST - ON GEIGER *GOOGER ROOTER BAGGER OLE!*

WAIT--- --- WHO YOU?

A LI'L PLANT LICE...

NAME OF GEIGER?

IS YOU RADIO-ACTIVE?

NOT SO ACTIVE. NAME IS FRED AN' IT'S ON TH' WAITIN' LIST AT *NBC* AND *CBS* ... BUT NOBODY IS USIN' CRICKET IMITATIONS THESE DAYS.

"B's GIVE ME A IDEA --- C'MERE CAP'N LA FEMME.

HOLE OPEN THE BOX, SON --- BEES IS MIGHTY NIGH AS SMALL AS THE ADAMS BUGS AND THEY IS A PECK MORE EXPLOSIVE --- WE GONE CONSTRUCT A "B" BOMB 'STEAD OF A "A" BOMB.

NOW WE IS REALLY GOT A BOMB ---- A BEE BOMB WITH A WHOLE BEE-HIVE IN IT.

WE IS LEADIN' THE LEAGUE - I WILL HELP YOU DOWN THE LADDER, DOC.

YOWP!

AT LAST! WE CAPTURED THE LUNCH.

AND NOW, MR. SMART CATS, I IS GOT THE BIG OL' LUNCH AN' YOU CAN WATCH ME DEE-VOUR THE ----

NO --- WAIT!

LIKE THE MAN SAY, SON, WAIT.

I FIGGER IT BETTER TO DEE-VIDE BEFORE YO' DEE-VOUR --- RATHER'N GO TO ALL THAT FUSS AFTER YOU EATS IT, BROWN EYES.

WALT KELLY

61

62

MY LOVE IS A ROSE OUR VIOLENCE BLUE; A YOUNG MAN'S FANCY AND SO, DEAR, ARE YOU

OLD CORNISH AIR

THIS LADY WHOM YOU WOO, PORKY, IS IT THE SAME WHO USED TO PLAY AT SEE-SAW WITH YOU?

NO! EVERY TIME I WAS LOW MAN ON THAT *TEETER BOARD*, SHE WOULD SLIDE DOWN TO *MY* END OF THE SEE-SAW.

WHOOSH! DOWN SHE *SWEPT!* HIT ME IN THE MIDDLE OF A FOUR BAR *DRONE* SOLO (WHICH I RATHER FANCIED)---WELL, FRIENDS, *THAT* TOOK THE WIND OUT OF *MY* BAGPIPES, I *MUST SAY!*

NOT ONLY *THAT*---BUT IN HER RECKLESS HASTE, SHE *PUNCHED* TWO TICKETS TO THE *1938 WARE COUNTY FAIR* THAT I'D BEEN SAVING IN MY HAT FOR A *RAINY DAY.*

WHAT A SORRY WASTE

THIS *NEW LADY ACQUAINTANCE* IS A DELIGHT TO THE EYE, POGO--- A VERY *QUEEN* OF LOVELINESS!

GEE GOSH

MMP!

HER *VOICE* IS THAT OF AN *ANGEL*--HER *EYES* ARE LIKE *DEEP FOREST POOLS....*

HOT DOG!

BOY!

HOLD IT! *INTERLUDE OF SMALL ACTIVITY BACKSTAGE.*

WINNIPEG WAS OPEN, THE BURST AGAIN TO SING, OH, WORSE THAN THAT A *DANISH DITCH* WAS *TWO-BY-FOUR* THE *KING*.

YOU'RE *HIRED*.

YOU WANT US TO *START*?

WHAT'LL WE *PLAY*?

START FOR *AUSTRALIA* AND *PLAY DOMINOES!*

PORKYPINE DIN'T LIKE THE SONG US *SERENADERS* WROTE IN ORDER TO HELP HIM *COURT* HIS *LADY FRIEND*---LET'S PRACTICE A NEW ONE.

RIGHT

OH, THE PARSNIPS WERE *SNIPPING* THEIR *SNAPPERS*--- WHILE THE *PARSLEY* WAS *PARCELING* THE *PEAS* --- AND *PARSING* A *SENTENCE* FROM *HANDLE* TO *HAND* WAS A *HORNET* WHO HUMMED WITH THE *BEES*.

OH---

WAIT*!* WAIT! SOMETHIN' IS PLUGGED UP MY *SOUSAPHONE.*

AW, YOU'RE *FLAT* ANYHOWS.

NOT *HALF* AS *FLAT* AS *YOU* GONE BE IF YOU *DOESN'T* STOP SNEAKIN' INTO *REHEARSALS!*

MI MI MI

70

WHY, 'ALLO TODAY! HOW EES ZEE *POGOS* TODAY AN' ZEE HOUND DOG *TODAY?*

HA! 'LO

I DON'T RIGHTLY SEE *WHAT* PORKY AN' ALBERT SEE IN---HUH---HMMM

PHOO--- NEITHER DO I--- ---UM---

♫ OH, MISS *HEPZIBAH!* ♪ UGH!

OH MISS ♫ *HEPZIBAH!* ✱OWD! ♪

OH, *GOODEE!* YOU EES SO SWEET, GARÇONS, TO FIND ZEE HONKYCHEEF OF MY FRAN', *MADAM BEAVAIR* WHO I HAVE LOST EET FOR HER!

AS I WAS SAYIN', *I* DON'T SEE SO MUCH IN MISS MAM'SELLE HEPZIBAH; *NOTHIN'* TO RAVE ABOUT.

COURSE NOT COURSE NOT COURSE NOT COURSE NOT

SORT OF DAMP OUT TODAY, POGO. GUESS WE'RE IN FOR A SPELL OF RAIN.

THAT SO? I ISN'T REALLY NOTICED.

WHAT'S WRONG WITH *MILWAUKEE?*

HERE NOW, **THAT'S** NOT EXACTLY A *FAIR* QUESTION!

I CAN'T WAIT TO GIT TO *MILWAUKEE* SO'S WE CAN START BEIN' COWBOYS AN' SHERIFFS AN' RUSTLERS.

AN' MAKE A *MILLION DOLLARS* LIKE **HOOPAROUND CASSOWARY** SELLIN' **COWBOY** *PARTS!*

COWBOY PARTS?

SURE! *THAT'S* THE MODERN GOLD MINE--- SPARE PARTS FOR COWBOYS: **WHISTLES, GUNS, COOKIES, COMIC BOOKS,** ETC.

THE MODERN COW POKE LIVES OFF THE FAD OF THE LAND, SON.

I MUST **REMEMBER** THAT **EXCELLENT WITTICISM** WHEN I WRITE MY **AUTOBIOLOGY.**

SAY, BUG, WHICH WAY TO *MILWAUKEE*?

LET'S SEE--- IT'S ABOUT LUNCH TIME--- SO MILWAUKEE SHOULD BE OVER THAT WAY---

OR, *NO* --- IT'S **WEDNESDAY** AND THERE'S NO PIANO LESSON. SO MILWAUKEE WOULD BE MORE IN THE **OTHER** DIRECTION BEHIND THAT THICKET.

AUKEE BUST

THE BUG SAID THAT MILWAUKEE WAS OFF BEHIND *THIS THICKET!*

HEY, **SEMINOLE SAM!** WHERE'S MILWAUKEE?

UP HERE--- PLAYIN' MICHIGAN WITH ME--OOP! *THAT'S MY CARD!*

YOU MEAN THE MILWAUKEE WE IS FOUND IS A LI'L *BUG?*

YEP, **MILWAUKEE MOE!** HE CAN'T BE SEEN BY THE *ORDINARY NAKED EYE!*

DO I GOTTA PUT A SET OF UNDERWEARS, LI'L SOCKS AN' A DERBY ON MY NUDE EYEBALL JUS' TO SEE A *PLAIN BUG?*

THIS IS NO MERE TINY BUG--- *MILWAUKEE IS A MENTAL GIANT*--- SUBTRACT **TWO FROM TWO,** MILWAUKEE--- (WHAT'S HE SAY, ALBERT?)

NOTHIN'

ZOUNDS! WHAT A BRAIN! THE RIGHT ANSWER IN THE **TWINK** OF AN EYE! AN INTELLECTUAL GOLIATH!

I'VE HAD AS MUCH TALK ABOUT YOUR BUG AS I CAN STAND--- *I AM HEADING WEST AGAIN!*

YOU, A **COW,** GOING **WEST?** WHY, THAT'S **COW** COUNTRY OUT **THERE!**

NATURALLY! I'M ALL SET--- *I AM A COW!* A FULL BLOODED, FOUR LEGGED, SQUARE RIGGED COW!

OKAY---HAVE IT YOUR WAY--- LET'S HEAR YOU BELLER LIKE A COW.

GLADLY--- **MEOW!**

MEOW? M-E-O-W? *THAT'S A COW NOISE?*

WELL, IT GOES *SOMETHING* LIKE THAT--- I HAVEN'T REALLY HAD MUCH TIME TO PRACTICE.

86

I'LL TRY ONCE MORE--
MEOW!

SORRY... YOU'D BETTER FACE IT AND TAKE THAT JOB IN FORT MUDGE CHASING MICE.

MY! MY! ARE MICE FIERCE?

NOT *EXACTLY*--- THEY'RE MORE *MOODY-LIKE!* YOU'LL NEVER HAVE A DULL MOMENT.

AH, THERE GOES A GOOD KID--- COULDN'T MAKE OUT AS A COW. WAS HEADIN' WEST FOR THE **BIG TIME** TOO.

DIDN'T HAVE THE VOICE, EH? KEPT MOOING, *"MEOW."*

YEP---AN' NOW IT'S BACK TO A HEART-BROKEN JOB AS A CAT.

MOOS IN TWO SYLLABLES, EH?

WELL, CHASING MICE WILL BE FUN.

HOW 'BOUT CAT FOOD? COWS DON'T EAT *MICE*---DOES SHE DRINK MILK?

GEE--- I NEVER THOUGHT TO ASK.

MUCH ADIEU
ABOUT NOTHING

LOOKY.' A STRANGER IN OUR MIST.'

A LI'L CARRIER PIGEON.'

COULD YOU MOVE YO' TAIL-BONE, SIR--? I IS TOO FOOT SORE TO **WALK** 'ROUND IT.

WHY DOESN'T YOU **FLY?** YOU IS A FLYIN' TYPE CRITTUR.

SHORT WINGS.

WHAT BRINGS YOU TO THE SWAMP, PIGEON?

MY PO' NATURAL-BORN, OVER-WORKED FEET BONES.

NO---I MEANS **WHY** IS YOU HERE?

I'M ONE OF THEM THINGS WHAT'S ALL THE RAGE---A **MAN** WITH A **MESSAGE!**

WHAT IS IT?

THAT'S WHAT THEY **DIN'T** DONE TOLE ME.

IT'S SUCH A **POW'FUL** SECRET NOBODY DIN'T EVEN DONE TELL ME **WHO'S** IT FOR.

BEEN KEEPIN' IT IN MY SHOE AN' IT'S KIND OF WORED OUT --- ONLY *PART* LEFT IS THE NAME.

ANYBODY EVER HEAR OF A GENERAL WHAT GO BY NAME OF LEE --- *ROBERT E. LEE*, THAT IS?

H'LO, POGO.

HEY! OL' ALBERT AN' ME FOUND A **MAN WITH A MESSAGE** --- A OL' CARRIER PIGEON WITH SHORT WINGS --- HE'S A WALKIN' TYPE BIRD AN' HE WORED RIGHT ON THRU THE NOTE PAPER, 'COUNT OF HE TOTED IT IN HIS SHOE.

HE WALKED HISSELF RIGHT OUT OF A JOB---NOW HE ISN'T GOT NO MESSAGE 'CEPT A HOLE!

PSST! THERE'S YOUR CHANCE!

MY CHANCE?

YOU'RE TIRED OF CARRYIN' THE MAIL--- YO' FEETS HURT---NOW YOU CAN SELL OUT! SELL ALL YO' MAIL TO THE PIGEON. LET HIM GO INTO THE POST OFFICIN' BUSINESS!

OL' PIGEON HERE IS FRESH OUTEN MESSAGES SO HE ALSO OUT OF A JOB.

TODAY IS HIS OPERA-TOONITY.

YEP, I, THE NATURAL-BORN MAILMAN, IS GOT SOME MIGHTY HIGH-CLASS MAIL AT LOW CLASS RATES!

I'LL TAKE THIS ONE--- IT GOT A MIGHTY HIGH-TONE SMELL ON IT.

FOOF! I NEVER WAS MUCH TOOK WITH ANYBODY WHO GOOD SMELLIN' MAIL WAS FOR!

TAIN'T WHO FANCY SMELLIN' MAIL IS FOR--- IT'S WHO IT'S FROM---I'LL JES' RETURN THIS FOR INSUFFOOCIENT POSTAGE.

90

HAH!

HOW 'BOUT THEM YOU USES WHEN YOU **WHANGS** YO' **FINGERBONE** WITH A **HAMMER?**

OH... *THEM?*

LIES! EVASION! SUBTER-FUSE!

AT LAST HE GONE SWEAR HE **ISN'T** MEANT NO **DISRESPECT** TO OUR SOVEREIGNTY.

I SWEARS: GOSH-A-MIKKLE DICKLE PICKLE DAG NAG AN'...

LOUDER!

AN' TAKE OFF YO' HAT!

DAG NAB YOU BLACKSTABBIN' BAGSTAGGERED OL' GOATS ANYHOWS!

ISN'T WE BEEN MORE SWORED *AT* THAN *WITH*?

I NOT SURE IS OUR NATIONAL HONOR BEEN VINDICATED OR **LIN**QUIDATED.

THAT OUGHT TO TAKE CARE OF *YOU* AN' THE SWEARIN'!

MISS MAM'ZELLE HEPZIBAH, I IS BRUNG OVER MY FIANNCY.

AH! TRÈS BON! YOU SHOULD HAVE ZE SOCIETY WEDDING WEETH ZE GOWN AN' ZE FLOWAIR, NON?

YAS, INDEED! I GOT A TRAIN FOR THE WEDDIN'.

YOU GOTTA TRAIN? WHAT THIS GONE BE? A CHAMPEENSHIP FIGHT?

STOP SITTIN' THERE SOAKIN' YOUR FEET IN THE TEA AND HELP ME GET READY FOR OUR WEDDIN'.

BUT THIS IS THE BEST THING I'VE TRIED YET FOR MY TIRED FOOTS!

COME, MEESTAIR PEA-JEAN, OBSERVE! EEN THE SOUTH ZE GENTLEMEN REESENT WHEN A MAN DOES NOT GO THRU WEETH A MARRIAGE!

THEY AIN'T GONE RESENT IT HALF SO MUCH IF I DON'T DO IT AS I DOES DO IF I DO DOES!

HA, BUT YOU MAY FIND YOURSELF IN ZE DUEL!

IF I DO, IT WON'T BE ME.

FOOF! YOU HAVE NO FLAIR! YOU'RE NOT ZE DASHING TYPE!

GIMME A OPEN ROAD AND YOU GONE SEE SOME DASHIN' WHAT GOT A REAL FLAIR ON IT.

98

99

EVAIRSING EES ALL HOKAY! I HAVE FIND ZE CHOMPEEN WHO EES TO DEFEND ZE **HONAIR** OF ZE **COWARDLY** PEA-JEAN WHO EES **RUN AWAY!**

AN' THE **HONOR** OF THE **SWAMP** WHAT WAS **INSULTED** BY THE **CRAVEN BUM** IN THE **FIRST PLACE** WILL BE DEFENDED BY OUR **OTHER** CHAMPEEN--?

RIGHT.

AN' **POGO** IS THE CHAMPEEN WHO GONE DEFEND **OUR** HONOR AN' **MIZ BEAVER'S** HONOR WHO WAS INSULTED BY THE PIGEON BY NOT MARRYIN' HER.

RIGHT.

WHO'S THE CHAMPEEN WHAT GONE DEFEND THE **PIGEON'S** HONOR?

WHO ELSE?! *MEEZ BEEVAIR!*

YOU MEANS **POGO**, WHO **DON'T WANT** TO FIGHT A DUEL IN THE **FIRST PLACE**, **GOTTA** DEFEND THE **HONOR** OF **MIZ BEAVER** WHO WAS---

---INSULTED BY THE *PIGEON* WHO RAN AWAY TO **WASHINGTON** TO BE A **BALL-HEADED IGGLE** AN' THAT LEAVES **NOBODY** FOR POGO TO **DUEL**, SO *SOMEBODY---*

---GOT TO STAND AN' UPHOLD THE **MIZZABLE PIGEON'S** HONOR AN' FIGHT POGO, AN' THE *ONLY ONE* **WILLIN'** TO DO IT IS---

NATURELLEMENT, MEEZ BEEVAIR!

IT DON'T MAKE *SENSE!*

SENSE! PHAUGH! WE SPEAK OF *HONAIR, M'SIEUR, NOT SENSE!*

WELL, **POGO,** IS YOU ALL READY FOR THE **DUEL?**

YEP, I IS PRACTICED *FIRIN'* THE GUN, BUT DIDN'T GET TO **HIT** NOTHIN' YET 'CAUSE LOUD NOISES SCARES ME AN' I IS BEEN **FEARED** TO PULL THE TRIGGER.

AT AIMIN' IT THOUGH, I IS A NATURAL BORNED *EXPERT!*

YO' **LUNCH** WHAT IS ALL PACKED FO' THE *BIG DAY* IS MIGHTY **INNERESTIN'.**

SINCE YOU IS FIGHTIN' THE DUEL AT DAWN, *YOU MIGHT NOT NEED NO LUNCH COME NOON*... SO I'LL KEEP IT 'TIL WE FINDS OUT AN' SAVE **YOU** THE WORRY OF IT.

TURTLE, HOW CAN I *EVER* THANK YOU?

AH! IT WORKS JES' GREAT!

AN' WHO'S IN IT, ALBERT?

PLING!

THE **PARTY** WHAT OWNS IT IS THE **PARTY** WHAT'S IN IT AN' THE **PARTY** WHAT'S IN IT IS THE **PARTY** WHAT GONE WEAR IT TO THE DUEL AN' *THAT PARTY* IS THE **PARTY** WHAT GONE **PERFORM** OPPOSITE YOU **IN** THE DUEL.

US KIN WEAR WHAT US PLEASES.

THE **BIG DUEL DAY** IS HERE---AN' EVER'BODY IS HERE TO WISH POGO **GOOD B'**...UH--I MEAN GOOD **LUCK!**

BIG DUEL TODAY

HERE Y'ARE---BALLOONS, FAVORS, SAN'WICHES---SCORECARDS---Y'CAN'T TELL THE PLAYERS WITHOUT A SCORECARD, SON.

I CAN-- I'M *IN* IT.

Now then, take your guns, folks.

KAPOW!
KAPOW!
KAPOW!
KAPUT!

THERE HE IS ...... HE GOT *FLANG OVERBOARDS.*

HOW *LUCKY* FOR *ME!* IF I'D OF *GOT* HIM I WOULD OF *WON* AN' MY *HONOR* WOULD *STILL* BE SULLIED AN' *I* WOULD FEEL *JES' AWFUL!*

SO WOULD I.

CONGRATULATIONS! POGO, YOU IS DEFENDED MY HONOR *FIRST RATE.*

WHAT WAS THIS ALL ABOUT?

YOU IS KINDA GOT *ME---* MEBBE CAP'N CHURCHY KIN EXPLAIN.

WELL, MA *BOBBA* MUMF WUMFA GOOBBIS OGGUL DUBBIS---AN' *THEN* WHOSIS UMFGU BOVVIL *DOBBLE*...

BUT WUBBLIG GROMPIS GOO HOGGER AND BUFFIG MUM GOBBLIN! SNMP?

THAT THE WAY YOU SEE IT?

EXACTLY.

EVERY DAY HAS ITS DOG

108

110

111

"WE FOUND HIM FLOATIN' IN A SACK."

"THAT WAS *OUR* MISTAKE --- WE PUT HIM IN THERE TO GET RID OF ---- *A-HEM!*"

"BEFORE WE FOUND OUT THERE WAS A BIG REWAR--- HEY--*OW!*"

A-HEM!

"FOR A MAN WHAT ISN'T MAKIN' ANY MUSIC YOU SHO' IS BEATIN' OUT A MESS OF TIME THERE, STRANGER"

"ALBERT, THESE TWO STRANGERS IS UN-VESTIGATIN' THE LOST PUP-DOG MYSTERY. THEY ASKS IF YO' HAD ANYTHIN' *UN-USUAL* HAPPEN LATELY ---?"

"WELL--WHEN I WAS ASLEEP I HAD A REAL-LIKE *DREAM!* SEEM SOMEBODY FED ME *SOMETHIN'* AN' I SAYS TO MYSELF, ASLEEP LIKE, *'MAN, THAT IS TASTY!'*"

WHAT!?
IN ---*YOUR*---*SLEEP*---YOU---*ATE*---*SOMETHIN'*-- AN' --- IT ---- *WAS* ---*WAS*-- *WAS*----Tasty?

"SURE WAS!"

"THE LI'L' DOG CHILE WHICH WAS SO LOVEABLE -- DEAR AND SWEET--WHICH *DIS*APPEARED *AND* VANISHED ---*THAT WAS A LITTLE DOG WHAT GO BY NAME OF 'TASTY!'*"

114

AND, WHILE THE SEARCH GOES ON..

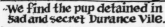
··We find the pup detained in sad and secret Durance Vile.

Looking for the lost dog, *eh?* **Well!** *Every-one thinks* **Albert ate** *the poor lad~* **The Investigators** *express* **grave** *fears ~~~ O! I shall* **demand** *custody of the* **Child** *! No cannibal is a fit guardian.*

HOW CAN **YOU** BE IN CHARGE OF A PUP WHAT IS **ALREADY** **ET** BY ALBERT?

~ Well! There's duplicity for you! **See how** *cunning and under~handed he is?* ~~

117

A LI'L' DOG DISAPPEARS NEAR A CRITTUR WHAT COMES FROM A FAMBLY WHAT **EATS ANYTHING.** --- AND *THAT* LI'L' DOG IS **NEVER SEED AGAIN.**

WHAT'S A BODY TO THINK?

I HEARD YO' LAST *REE-MARK,* PORKY --- LET'S **FACE FACTS!** *STOP SHILLY-SHALLYIN'!* THE CRITTUR YOU MENTION *GOTTA* BE GUILTY --- HE JUS' MUST OF *ET* THE PUP DOG --- AN' I DON'T CARE **WHO** HE IS!

IT'S ABOUT TIME **JUSTICE** WAS DID --- IF SOMEBUDDY *ATE* THAT PUP DOG, **SOMEBODY** GOTTA *PAY!* THE GUILTY SHOULD BE PUNISHED! --- *DAG BLAG IT!* STOP DRAGGIN' YO' TAIL, POGO---

OOOMPH!

LET THE BLAME FALL WHERE SHE MAY, ALBERT?

Y BONDS

THE LIBERTY BELLE

WHERE-*EVER* SHE MAY! I IS FIRM! WHO DOES THE UNVESTIGATORS SUSPECK? *WHERE* DO THE FINGER-BONE POINT? *WHO'S THE ONE? IT MATTER NOT --- BUT* **WHO?**

WELL,

HE'S IN THIS BOAT.

THE LIBERTY BELLE

AS ALBERT'S LAWYER, I GOTTA QUESTION ALL THE JURY MEMBERS, MIZ LIMPKIN; I HOPES YOU HASN'T DECIDED THAT ALBERT'S GONE BE FOUND **GUILTY** LIKE MOST FOLKS HAS.

I MOST CERTAINLY HAS **NOT** DECIDED HE'S GONE BE FOUND **GUILTY**.

GOOD FOR YOU, MIZ LIMPKIN.

'COURSE I MUS' SAY, ON THE OTHER HAND, I CERTAINLY **HAS** MADE UP MY MIND THAT HE COULD **NEVER** BE FOUND **"NOT GUILTY"**.

ALL RIGHT, LET'S GIT GOIN' WITH TH' TRIAL! COURT'S OPEN FOR BUSINESS.

IS THE JURY READY WITH THE GUILTY VERDICK YET? LET'S NOT DILLY DALLY.

JUST FOR LAUGHS, OWL, LET'S ASK A FEW QUESTIONS FIRST.

BUY BONDS

THE LIBARTY BELLE

HIT THIS SIGN WITH A BATTED BALL AND WIN A NEW SUIT.

SMOKE OLD SHOES

125

126

WELL, YOU CONVINCED *ME!* BUT---- *WHO'S EATIN'* AT ME?

JUST A MINION OF THE LAW... FANGIN' A FOE.

TELL THAT LI'L OL' MINION TO **STOP** TAKIN' **UNCIVIL LIBERTIES** WITH MY TAILBONE BEFORE A *EX*PERT FANGER PUT THE FINGER ON *YO' BOTH.*

In the secret dungeon ~

WELL, WELL! HOW'S THE BOY THIS MORNING? I BROUGHT YA A COMICAL-BOOK TO CHEER YA UP.

THIS IS **GOOD** CLEAN FUN-- SEE, THE HATCHET MURDERER DOES ALL HIS WORK IN THE BATHTUB---*WHAT COULD BE CLEANER?* NOW HE STUFFS GRANDMA, ALIVE, INTO THE DOC'S STERILIZER! VERY TIDY.

GOOD WORK, KID --- YOU'LL PROB'LY GROW UP TO BE A GREAT EDITOR.

REMINDS ME OF A TIME I JUMPS SHIP IN LIVERPOOL AN' HERE'S A BIG STUPID CAT IN A' GREEN GROCER'S SHOP---- HA, WELL, I----- *SAY, WE MUST BE IN A EARTHQUAKE!*

Be of Good Cheer

YOU SEE WHY WE DIDN'T FIND A CONFESSION IN THOSE LANGUAGES, JURY? *ALBERT* CAN'T WRITE IN THOSE LANGUAGES!

A TELLING POINT!

OH, HE'S GUILTY!

WHO?

IN *FACT*, FRIENDS... I DON'T B'LIEVE OL' ALBERT COULD WRITE A CONFESSION IN *PLAIN ENGLISH!*

AH! HA!

AW, I COULD TOO!

HERE'S HOUN'DOG'S HOUSE ~ MEBBE HE CAN HELP ALBERT.

SPSSST!

WHAT YOU HIDIN' OUT HERE FOR, BEAU-REGARD?

SOMEBODY TOOK MY COUSIN'S LI'L BOY DOG FROM OUT FORT MUDGE. I IS WATCHIN' THAT HOUSE ---- NOTICE THEM TRACKS GOIN' OUT? AND *NONE* GOIN' BACK IN?

THAT IS *PLAIN* SUSPICIOUS! SO I WAITIN' FOR THE CRITTUR TO COME BACK.

BUT--- IT'S YOUR OWN HOUSE, HOUN'DOG.

NO WONDER I ISN'T SEED NOBODY COME BACK! I BEEN OVER HERE ALL THE TIME AN' COULDN'T GO BACK MY-SELF AND IF I DID GO BACK I WOULDN'T OF SEED NOBODY BECAUSE I WOULD-N'T OF BEEN HERE TO SEE ME GO BACK 'CAUSE IT WOULD OF BEEN *ME* GOIN' BACK AT THE TIME.

GOIN'?

YEP. WAY WAY BACK.

131

132

134

TEN FOOT POLL TAX

LOOKY! LOOKY! A POO-RADE!

VOTE FOR OWL

A VOTE FOR O.W.

YOU OUT TO GIT *EELECTED* TO SOMETHIN' OWL? WHAT'S YOU FOR?

I IS FOR *ME* MOSTLY, BUT ALSO FOR **WIMMIN AND CHILLUN SUFFRAGE.**

YOU DON'T GIT **MY** VOTE --- WIMMIN AN' CHILLUN **SUFFERS** PLENTY AS IT GO NOW.

IF JOKES COULD *VOTE,* THAT ONE WOULD OF CAST A BALLOT FOR **TIPPECANOE TYLER!**

IS A VOTE FOR Y-O-U

Ahem! Some of the voters are urging Me to run.

WHICH WAY? WHAT YOU BEEN UP TO, DEACON?

VOTE FOR OWL

Elections are coming up... These are perilous times -- We need strong hands -- and I have always had a flair for foreign Relations

135

Panel 1: I ALLUS THOUGHT YOU WERE **ONE HUNNERD PERCENT** AMERICAN?

VOTE FOR OWL

Panel 2: Naturally~ What else? Especially Today ~~~ as things go.

Panel 3: THEN, HOW COME YOU GOT SUCH A BIG OL' **FLAIR** FOR YOUR FOREIGN **REELATIONS?**

VOTE FOR OWL

Panel 4: Hold still, Friend, I have a **Martial** plan of my own.

WAIT 'TIL AFTER ELECTIONS, DEACON.

Copy down my election speech, Pogo: Ladies and Gentlemen, if you elect me, I promise that the War of 1812 will be but a memory.

I promise Peace with Mexico by Christmas or 50 for 40 and fight ~~~~ And I pledge to never impede the flow of the **Mississippi River.**

WHAT IN THE WORLD IS **THAT** ALL ABOUT?

I am a man of **Integrity,** Pogo, I only make promises I can keep.

MAN, YOU CAN SURE **KEEP THOSE**--- AND YOU BETTER KEEP 'EM DOWN THE CELLAR IN THE COOL SO'S THEY DOESN'T SPOIL.

NOW, BEFORE I CLOSE MY **BRILLIANT CAMPAIGN** SPEECH TO THE FRENZIED CHEERS OF YOU **ADMIRERS** --- *IS THEY **ANY** QUESTIONS?*

YES, **WHAT** IS YOU' RUNNIN' FOR?

VOTE FOR OWL

HMM --- **WELL!** A **VERY** GOOD QUESTION --- WELL, I'M RUNNIN' FOR **PUBLIC OFFICE** ON ACCOUNT I IS GONE BE **SOMEBODY IMPORTANT!** --- INSTEAD OF A COMMON ORNERY TYPE OF LOW LIFE LIKE ---

LIKE **WHO?**

WELL --- UM ---

LIKE ORNERY CITIZENS?

SO TO SPEAK --- **SO** TO SPEAK.

THE LOW TYPE GITS UP TO BAT **SOON** OWL, THEN YOU'LL FIND OUT WHO'S **REALLY** IMPORTANT.

VOTE FOR OWL

GOSH --- POGO TALKIN' 'BOUT **US.**

NATURAL

COME WASH YO' FACE AN' PUT ON A CLEAN COLLAR --- WE GOIN' TO **VOTE.**

VOTE!? I ISN'T GONE DISCOMFORT **MY SELF** JES' TO VOTE FOR A PARCEL OF **MUTTON HEADS!**

WELL, I IS ALL DRESSED UP AND IS PACKED A NICE LUNCH --- AN' *BESIDES IT'S YOUR* **DUTY!**

HAH! I OWE **NOTHING** TO THESE POLITICAL **POLTROONS!** I WOULDN'T VOTE FOR 'EM FOR **DOG CATCHER!**

DOG CATCHER.!? WHAT *AM* I SAYING?!

IF YOU DON'T WANT TO VOTE *FOR* SOMEBODY, YOU CAN VOTE *AGAINST* SOMEBODY.

WAIT A MINUTES WHILE I *WASH MY MOUTH OUT WITH SOAP*, THEN I'LL GO *VOTE AGAINST EVERY DOG CATCHER IN SIGHT!*

SURE, VOTIN' *THIS* YEAR IS KIND OF GUARANTEEIN' YO'SELF YOU'LL BE *FREE* TO VOTE *NEX'* YEAR.

POGO, OF ALL THE VOTES IN THE BOX *NOBODY GOT MORE'N ONE!* WHY DIN'T YOU VOTE FOR ME?

OR ME?

I VOTED FOR *PORKY* AND I 'SPECT *HE* MUST OF VOTED FOR *ME*--- EVIDENTLY BOTH OF *YOU* VOTED FOR YOUR *OWN* SELFS.

BUT OF COURSE!

WHAT ELSE?

OH, WELL--- WE NEVER *DID* DECIDE WHAT *ANYBODY* WAS RUNNIN' FOR ANYWAYS.

IF I'D OF WON, I'D OF *NAMED IT!*

ME TOO!

A STIRRING TALE

142

BEWITCHED, BOTHERED AND BEMILDRED

WELL, MR. BAT, IF YOU WANTS TO RENT THAT *VACANCY* YOU *CAN---*

HOW 'BOUT THIS *DRAFT?*

IT STOPS WHEN YOU CLOSES THE DOOR.

I'LL TRY IT.

HOW'S THAT?

GREAT!

AH, *WHOOMP!?*

HEY! I ISN'T GONE TAKE THIS PLACE IF IT GOT NOISY NEIGHBORS!

I *RENTED* THIS SPACE INSIDE YO' *MOUTH* FROM YO' NEPHEW, ALBERT, AN', BY JING, I IS GONNA *STAY!*

I WAS HERE *FIRST!*

SQUATTERS RIGHTS GOT *NOTHIN'* TO DO WITH IT!

WELL, I ISN'T GONNA HAVE NO BATS LIVIN' *INSIDE MY HEAD!*

UNCLE ALBERT IS TRYIN' TO EVICT A BAT.

146

147

149

COULDN'T YOU **AUDIBLE BOY BIRD WATCHERS** TAKE YOUR BUSINESS *ELSEWHERE?* EVERY WHERE WE LOOKS, WE SEES **BLUE EYE BALLS.**

WE IS **ONLY** DOIN' OUR NATURAL BORN DUTY.

COULDN'T *YOU,* AS OUR **LANDLORD,** DO SOMETHIN' ABOUT **PEEKIN' TOMS?**

NO.' I IS GONE BE A **AUDIBLE BOY BIRD WATCHER** MYSELF.

PHOO! WE IS BEIN' STARED TO DEATH--- *BACK TO CARLSBAD!*

WE IS **ALL** LEAVIN'.

JEST A DOGBONED MINUTE.' YOU SWEEP OUT IN THERE 'FORE YOU GOES.'

WHEN ALBERT **DISPOSSESSED** US UNFORTUNATE BAT CRITTURS IT LEFT US **TEMPORARILY** AT **LEISURE.**

AN' WHEN *YOU,* THE **BOY BIRD WATCHERS SOCIETY,** STARTED *WATCHIN' US*--- IT WAS A INSULT---US **BATS** IS USUAL THE ONES ON THE OTHER END OF THE **SPY GLASS.**

151

152

153

154

161

162

LITTLE
POLTERGEISTS
SHOULD BE SEEN
AND NOT
HEARD

HE'LL *NEVER* LEARN TO HUNT! LOOK, HE'S POINTIN' ANOTHER *GRASS* HOPPER!

TADS ISN'T LIKE THEY WAS IN *MY* TIME.

YEP! IT'S PLAY! *PLAY! PLAY!* NEVER LEARN A TRADE—— *OH, NO!*

HE'S NO HUNTER.

SHHH

I TRY TO BE FAIR—I SAY: THE YOUTH TODAY ISN'T AS STUPID AS IT LOOKS——GIVE 'EM A CHANCE, I SAY——AND *THEN, BANG!*

THANKS, KID, HERE'S A LI'L TOKEN.

THIS HAPPENS—— WE'RE LOOKIN' FOR *BIRDS——* HE FINDS *CIGARS!*

TSK TSK TSK

170

"POLTERGEISTS MAKE UP THE PRINCIPAL TYPE OF SPONTANEOUS MATERIAL MANIFESTATION."

IT'S NOT EXACTLY A *ROUSER*. ---ANYTHING ELSE?

THAT'S ALL-- "*POLTERGEISTS ETC.---*"

SORRY; WHAT WOULD HE *EVER* DO FOR A *ENCORE*?

OH WELL, IT WAS A NICE DREAM.

AS LONG AS THE PUP-DOG CAN *TALK*, POGO, WE'RE GOING TO TAKE HIM ON A VAUDEVILLE TOUR.

NATURALLY, *I'LL* GO ALONG AS THE CHILD'S *GUARDIAN*--- I KNOW A FEW MAGIC TRICKS! WATCH *THIS* ONE--- I BREAK AN EGG INTO MY PLUG HAT---

I MIX IT THOROUGHLY--- *THEN*, WITHOUT HARMING THE HAT--- I----UH---WELL, WELL---HMM.---

YOUR TRICK *SMELLS* GOOD---IS IT *DONE* YET?

THE TEACHER SAY: "MY, AREN'T YOU *WARM?*" *(THAT'S ANOTHER TWO)* CHOMP---

RIGHT--- *SIX* UP TO NOW.

WELL? WHAT'S THE LAST LINE? THE *PAYOFF?* THE *BOFF?*

DING BING IT*!* I NEVER *CAN* REMEMBER THE LAST LINES OF JOKES--- CHOMP--- CHOMP---

POLTERGEISTS MAKE UP THE PRINCIPAL TYPE OF MATERIAL MANIFESTATION.

MAN! THAT LINE IS DRIVIN' ME CRAZY!

LET'S TEACH HIM HIS ACT.

NOW, WHEN WE SPEAK TO *YOU* AFTER THE MUSIC DIES DOWN, PUP, *YOU ANSWER:* " I JUST GOT BACK FROM THE ANIMAL SHOW*!*"

ALL RIGHT--- NOW YOU GOT IT*!*

♫♫ *HEAR THAT WHISTLE PUFF AND BLOW--♫ ♫ AS WE RIDE ON OUT OF BUFF·A·LO? ♫* HEHLO, JOE, WHAT D'YA KNOW?

POLTERGEISTS MAKE UP THE PRINCIPAL TYPE OF MATERIAL MANIFESTATION.

WHAT OUTSTANDING ACT CAN WE CLOSE OUR VAUDEVILLE PROGRAM WITH?---THE PUP DOG WILL SPEAK---AN' THEN----AN' THEN---

I'LL SING!

♪? Oh, wistfully blissly, Blithely I bless The sanguinely songing Of my sister Bess--- For longingly lightly And lissomely low The sowing of soda is ever so ··so ····· ♪

SO! THIS GIVES ME A GREAT IDEA FOR A FINISH! LIE DOWN, TURTLE!

LIKE SO?

LIKE SO.

HEY! NO FAIR! YOU CAN'T SAW A MUSICIAN IN HALF!

NOW, THE FIRST VAUDEVILLE TRICK THE PUP DOG WILL DO IS ADD A FEW SUMS--- NOW, HOW MUCH IS **ONE** AND **ONE**, LI'L DOG?

WURF! WURF!

GREAT! **TWO** BARKS! NOW, HOW MUCH IS----

WAIT! WAIT! NOT SO FAST! LET'S FIGGER OUT IF THE *FIRST* ANSWER IS RIGHT!

THE ATLANTA BELLE

174

175

176

WE DON'T WANT HIM TO GET THE PUP DOG BEFORE OUR TOUR STARTS. **YOOP!**

Who's after the Pup-Dog? You come along quietly, Albert.

Come along, Albert, You're fit bait for school and, as Truant Officer and Principal, I bring you in.

PHOO! I ISN'T GONNA RESIST, BUT I ISN'T GONNA DO MY OWN WALKIN'--- YOU IS GONE HAFTA *DRAG* ME THE WHOLE TWO MILES!

Harrump!

Hey! Why are you two sitting outside?

DOOR'S LOCKED.

IT'S SATURDAY--- NO SCHOOL.

A Merry Very Crispness

I KNOW IT'S FOUR O'CLOCK IN THE MORNING, POGO, BUT I THOUGHT I'D DROP BY. *CHRISTMAS* IS COMING AGAIN.

WHA'?

IT'S AN EVER PRESENT NUISANCE. I *DON'T LIKE ANYBODY* ---'CEPT ONE CRITTUR WHOM I DISLIKES *LESS* THAN MOST --- BEEN SAVING SOMETHIN' FOR HIM SINCE AUGUST.

A BLUNT INSTRUMENT?

A *DAISY!* IT'S YOURS --- DON'T THANK ME --- I HATE FAWN-ING, MAUDLIN SENTIMENT. YOU DON'T SEE DAISIES AT THIS TIME OF THE YEAR --- --- I ENJOYED THIS ONE, MAYBE YOU WILL, TOO.

KEEP IT AND HAVE A MERRY CHRISTMAS --- IF THE REST OF THE SWAMP CRITTURS DON'T LIKE YOU ANY BETTER THAN I DO, YOU WON'T GET A SIMPLE GOOD MORNING.

THANK YOU, ... YOU OL' PORKYPINE.

178

179